ILLUSTRATIONS BY EMMA DAVIES

Published in 2018 by Helen Exley ® LONDON in Great Britain.
Design, selection and arrangement are all © Helen Exley Creative Ltd 2018.
Illustrations by Emma Davis © Helen Exley Creative Ltd 2018.
Words by Pam Brown © Helen Exley Creative Ltd 2018.
Copyright © Helen Exley Creative Ltd 2018.
The moral right of the author has been asserted.

12 11 10 9 8 7 6 5 4 3 2 1
ISBN 978-1-78485-183-5

OTHER HELEN EXLEY BOOKS IN THIS SERIES
Thank you MUM - for everything   THANKS Dad!
Thank you for your LOVING ME   A Great Big Thank you
Thank you for your Kindness

Helen Exley ® LONDON, 16 Chalk Hill,
Watford, Hertfordshire, WD19 4BG, UK.
www.helenexley.com

Thank you to a Real FRIEND

BY PAM BROWN
PICTURES BY EMMA DAVIS

Helen Exley

Loved, needed,

You find yourself loved,
needed, missed.

missed.

Friendship is a sort of miracle.

Sharing a life

Sharer of anxieties.

Sharer of silly jokes.

Sharer of excitements.

Thank you for everything.

HAPPY DAY

You know a silly postcard
on a Monday morning
brightens the day
– the heart. The Universe!

No need to

You seem to know my needs
and answer them long before
I've put them into words.

speak

YOUR

Medicines may be necessary.
But your smile

SMILE

Flowers lift the heart.
is the best restorative of all.

Feeling so

I am so very ordinary.

good

Thank you
    for making me feel special.

LAUGHTER

The day started badly.
It was raining.
A fistful of bills.
A drift of circulars.
Gloom.
Doom.
But then you rang.
And made me laugh.

No friend has been

so constant.

No friend has been as true.
No friend has ever
meant as much as you.

MY GARDEN
IS BRIGHT
WITH PLANTS
THAT YOU
HAVE GIVEN ME.

YOUR GIFTS

ARE NOT PRACTICAL AND SENSIBLE.

THEY ARE ALWAYS FAR MORE.

THEY ARE GIFTS

OF IMAGINATION. THEY ARE

GIFTS OF DELIGHT.

Always There for

You are always there,
however distant,
constant as the Pole Star.
Unwavering in kindness
and concern – certainty
in an uncertain world.

me

You know
the words I need

You never say
what other people say.
You know the words
I need.

WE TWO

We don't need to ask each other.
We know the sort of play
the other likes, which books,
what music.
We know each other's most-loved
flower and scent. We know each
other's oddities. And so each meeting
is like coming home.

A MULTITUDE OF

You have rescued me
so often – from hysterical spin driers,
jammed doors, burnt cakes,
missed trains, hopeless love affairs.
How could I have survived
without you?

MINI DISASTERS!!

You have solved
so many of my calamities –
bless you for your grin
and your incredible,
all enveloping competence.

RESPECT

Thanks for giving and expecting
respect – and for making me feel
very, very necessary.

You give me
your time
— the most
generous gift
of all.

...knowing just when

to be silent

Thank you for knowing
when to be silent.
When to sit and simply hold my hand.

Quietly and calmly helping me

Thank you for very quietly
and very efficiently
getting me out of what seemed
like an inextricable mess.

Small things, silly things

It is not only the great kindnesses
that you have shown me – but
all the small and often silly things
that you have done to make me smile.
How dull life would
have been without you.

Small surprises – a bunch of
raggedy flowers on the doorstep
to start my day.
A fairy cake with a candle in the icing
on my birthday.
The book that I'd been searching for.
Fruit out of season. A ginger kitten.
– How did you know?

FREEDOM!

Thank you for
crazily outrageous days.
Which can encompass wicked
extravagances in fashion stores,
milk shakes by the sea,
gallery openings
and half-price sales.

TREATS

Friends carry a list in their heads:
clothes sizes, best-loved scents,
preferred shades, best-loved flowers
and edible delights.
And so find you Little Treats.

Every birthday,
every celebration, I can be certain
that at least one of my gifts
will be exactly what I hoped for.
The one from you.

Lonely

days

You dropped in for a chat,
  washed a few dishes, fed the cat.
Climbed those long stairs
  up to the lonely flat.
You did these things for me
    when I was in trouble,
  eased fear and pain.
      Thank you for that.

Friendship
can make
the unbearable bearable.

Thank you
for making me laugh
when I'd almost forgotten
how to.

Laughing

together

There is always
the endless traffic jam,
the closed café,
the deluge at the picnic,
the cancelled flight, the awful
meal we remember with a sigh,
a smile – a certain relish.
Friends can turn catastrophe
into happy memories.

ON MY SIDE

Thank you for telling me
   what I already knew in my heart,
but calmly, clearly, positively.
   So that I could take
      it from there.

Only you will do

There are times
when I have needed to tell someone
my fear, times when I have needed
someone to share a secret,
times when I have
needed someone to rejoice with me
over an achievement.
And those are the times when only
my friend will do.

Thank you for being the best
sounding board in the world.
I bring my half-baked plans to you,
my addled theories, muddled
resentments, shapeless dreams.
And come away with courage,
hope – and practicalities.

FRIENDS

Friends forgive.

When everyone else gives up
on me, you give a little sigh,
and set to untangling the mess
I've got myself into.

FORGIVE

Mercifully.

THERE FOR ME

Other people are sympathetic,
concerned, kind –
but never there.
You are – whenever I most need you.

Thank you for not
even noticing
     the chaos in the kitchen,
the wild disorder
     in the living room.

Blind to all my

faults!

As we grow older
the times we retell our tales increases
– thank you for pretending
you've never heard them before.

SMILES & LAUGHTER

Here's a bouquet of smiles
and giggles
and helpless laughter,
of tears and sighs and whispered secrets,
of triumphs and disasters
we have shared.
With gratitude and love.

All our days

...All the days we've walked
and talked together.
All the things we've shared,
our lives so interwoven that we can scarcely
think of life without each other.
Stay close – even if distance
should divide us.
I need your kindness and I need
your company.

...when I needed you

Thank you
for dropping everything
and coming
when I most desperately
needed you.

There are times in life
   when we most need friends.
On standby.
   Ready to do anything
or go anywhere.
      Thank you for doing,
   being, just that.

$\mathcal{T}$hank you for making me feel life is

worth having – whatever happens.

SOUL MATES

We are all fundamentally alone
– but a few people have the knack
of diminishing that isolation –
of reaching out to touch us.
Thank you for being such
a human being – thank you
for your companionship.

For a life

How does one say thank you for a life?
I thank you for always being there when
I most needed you – in sickness and
in sorrow. In days of wild rejoicing.
But most of all, I thank you for being
who you are. Constant and kind.
Patient and forgiving.
Sharing my journey – the best of
all companions.

What is a Helen Exley Giftbook?

Helen Exley Giftbooks cover the most powerful range of all human relationships: love between couples, the bonds within families and between friends.

No expense is spared in making sure that each book is as thoughtful and meaningful a gift as it is possible to create: good to give, good to receive.

You have the result in your hands. If you have loved it – please tell others! There is no power on earth like the word-of-mouth recommendation of friends.

Helen Exley® LONDON,
16 Chalk Hill, Watford, WD19 4BG, UK
www.helenexley.com